African Americans

in California

CALIFORNIA CULTURES SERIES

African Americans in California

Adam D. Parker

Toucan Valley Publications, Inc.

Available from: **Toucan Valley Publications, Inc.**
                         PO Box 15520
                         Fremont CA 94539-2620

                         www.toucanvalley.com

                         phone: (800) 236-7946
                         fax: (888) 391-6943
                         e-mail: editor@toucanvalley.com

About the *California Cultures Series*

America is a land of diversity. It has been called a melting pot, a salad bowl, a nation of immigrants. Of all the 50 states, California has the most cultural diversity in its population. According to the most recent figures released by the Bureau of the Census, California has 12% of the country's population, yet it has 34% of the Hispanic population and 38% of the Asian population. In 1996, California received 22% of all legal immigration to the United States, according to the California Demographic Research Unit. These immigrants came from Mexico, the Philippines, Vietnam, China, India, El Salvador, Taiwan, and many other countries.

The aim of the *California Cultures Series* is to promote understanding of diversity through the lives of California people. Other titles in the series:
> *Filipinos in California*
> *Japanese in California*
> *Mexicans in California*

About the Author

Adam D. Parker is a writer and editor who studied history as an undergraduate at the University of California at Berkeley and earned a Masters degree in history at the University of Wisconsin-Madison. An avid baseball fan and bridge player, Adam lives with his wife and their dog in the San Francisco Bay Area.

Contents

AFRICAN AMERICANS

IN CALIFORNIA

Americans have long seen California as a land of opportunity. For African Americans, California has often been a symbol of freedom and endless possibilities. Throughout much of American history, black people could expect better treatment in California than many other places. Nevertheless, the state has also been home to racial tensions and discrimination. The opportunities for black people have not always been the same as those available to whites.

California under Spain and Mexico

People of African ancestry have been part of the story of California for well over two centuries. In the late 18th century, Spain claimed California as one of its possessions, along with Mexico. "New Spain," as these North American possessions were called, was home to many people of African descent. Although some were slaves and a large number were descendants of slaves, people of African ancestry were readily accepted as part of the society.

Africans and mulattos (a term then used for people with some African ancestors) served as soldiers when San Diego and Montcrey were founded in 1769. They were also part of the De Anza Expedition that founded San Francisco in 1776. Of the 46 people who founded the city of Los Angeles in 1781, 26 had African roots. By 1790, one out of every five Spanish-speaking people who lived in California had some African heritage.

Mexico declared itself independent from Spain in 1821 and promised that all people, including Africans, would be treated fairly. As they had under Spanish rule, blacks continued to intermarry with Mexicans, Europeans, and California Indians. They also participated in government and went into many professions. Despite these good conditions, few African Americans entered California during this time. California was far away from the American South, and few black people could hope to escape that far West. Those who did come were sailors who left their ships while in California ports, or mountain men like James Beckwourth who explored and trapped in the West.

Enter the Americans

When James Marshall discovered gold at Sutter's Mill in 1848, the course of California history changed forever. Almost overnight, thousands upon thousands of people rushed to California in hopes of striking it rich.

California's legal status changed as well. After separating from Mexico the previous year, California adopted a state constitution that prohibited slavery in 1849. As part of the "Compromise of 1850," California was admitted into the union as a free state.

Some of the African Americans who entered the state during the gold rush did not come voluntarily. Even though California officially did not allow slavery, state officials did little to prevent it. By 1852, about 300 slaves searched for gold. Still others worked as servants.

Other African Americans entered California on their own. Some fugitive slaves successfully made the long journey and settled in Los Angeles. A larger number, however, came to northern California in search of gold. Like other gold seekers, only a few African Americans found much gold. Nevertheless, many men settled in California, especially in San Francisco and Sacramento.

White residents were suspicious of the African American newcomers. After the American takeover of California, officials repeatedly tried to pass laws to keep blacks from settling in California. Nevertheless, the African American population of the state rose from 1,000 to 5,000 during the 1850s. The new Californians faced laws that separated blacks and whites and did not allow African Americans to vote or to testify in trials involving whites.

Still, there were people in San Francisco who fought for the end of slavery and for equal rights for African Americans. In Los Angeles in 1856, Biddy Mason won her freedom from slavery through the court system. Another former slave, Mary Ellen Pleasant, sheltered fugitives and used her wealth and social position to fight for the rights of African Americans. Between 1855 and 1865, African Americans held four California Colored Conventions to demand equal treatment under the law.

With the end of the Civil War in 1865, passage of amendments to the United States Constitution ended slavery and guaranteed African Americans the right to vote and equal protection under the law. Life for African Americans in California improved. In San Francisco, African Americans owned boarding houses and restaurants. They published newspapers, built churches, and created social and political organizations.

As time passed, African Americans moved out of San Francisco into suburbs like Oakland and Berkeley. Oakland's position at the end of the Western Pacific Railroad meant that people who settled there would have jobs. The earthquake and fire that devastated San Francisco in 1906 caused even more African Americans to leave for the suburbs. Meanwhile, Los Angeles was growing quickly as people of all races settled in the city. By 1910, Los Angeles had more African Americans than any city in the state.

Migration and War

The Great Migration of the 1910s and 1920s further changed the face of California. Before this, 9 out of 10 African Americans lived in the South. Most of them worked on farms and all lived under laws that denied them equality and basic rights.

In the North, large cities needed people to work in their factories, in part because of the U.S. participation in World War I. African Americans left the South in record numbers. Most moved to northern cities; some made their way West. Some African Americans settled in San Francisco and Oakland, but most who came to the state at this time chose Southern California. From 1910 to 1930, the African American population of Los Angeles grew from 8,000 to 40,000 people.

The new Californians found both things to like and to hate about their new home. Wages were better than in the South and blacks faced less open hostility from their white neighbors. In Los Angeles, some African Americans entered the growing film industry.

But white Californians did not always welcome the newcomers. Whites used legal means to keep African Americans from living in "white" neighborhoods. Housing discrimination resulted in African Americans being crowded into a few neighborhoods.

While African Americans could find employment, they were usually forced to take jobs as unskilled laborers or domestic workers. These jobs were hard, low paying, and offered little chance for advancement. Even in the film industry, most African American actors were limited to playing unflattering roles that reflected stereotypes about them. This became a source of controversy in 1915 when the National Association for the Advancement of Colored People (NAACP) in California protested the showing of the racist movie *Birth of the Nation*.

The Great Depression hit America at the end of the 1920s. In 1931, one out of every three African Americans in Los Angeles was unemployed. All of that changed during World War II. By the time the United States entered the war in 1941, California was the center of the defense industry. One half of all the money spent to build the nation's guns, planes, and boats was spent in California. Building those things required more than just money, it required people. In 1941, President Franklin D. Roosevelt signed Executive Order 8802. This rule said that companies building things for the military could not discriminate against African American workers.

With so many jobs available, California had another population explosion. 340,000 African Americans entered California from 1940 to 1945, almost tripling the number of African Americans in the state.

The growth of Richmond, California, is an excellent example of the changes brought by the war. In 1940, Richmond was a small community with only 270 African Americans. During the war, it became an important shipbuilding center. The Kaiser company advertised throughout the South telling of the good jobs that could be found in Richmond. Eventually, the Kaiser shipyards employed 150,000 people, and one out of every six of them was African American. By the end of the war, Richmond had 14,000 African American residents.

As African Americans swelled California cities, they faced increased discrimination. Even with the good incomes provided by wartime work, they were often made to live in overcrowded neighborhoods. At work, the unions representing war workers forced African Americans to join the union (and pay dues), but did not allow them to vote on issues that concerned all workers. In one such case in Marin City, African American workers who protested were fired from their jobs. The California Supreme Court later rejected this discrimination.

The end of the war brought many challenges for African Americans. Fewer workers were needed. Returning soldiers filled many of the remaining positions. The overcrowded, urban "ghettos" into which many African Americans moved during the war quickly became unpleasant places in which to live. Many of California's African Americans faced uncertain futures.

California in Modern Times

In the last fifty years, African Americans have made many legal gains in California. In 1959, the state legislature outlawed discrimination against African Americans in hiring for jobs. A fair housing law was passed in 1963 and the California Supreme Court later ruled that landlords could not discriminate on the basis of race. Freed of this legal obstacle, middle-class African Americans increasingly left cities to move to the suburbs.

African Americans also had success at the ballot box. In 1962, Augustus Hawkins became California's first African American in Congress. Tom Bradley made history in 1973 by becoming mayor of Los Angeles, a position he held for two decades. Northern California leader Willie Brown became a powerful speaker of the California assembly and, in 1995, the mayor of San Francisco.

Some African Americans communities, however, still experienced discontent. In 1965, just one year after the Urban League named Los Angeles the best city in the country for blacks to live, a riot in the Watts section of the city showed citizens' anger at their treatment by the largely white police department. Decades later, when a video camera captured white police officers hitting an African American motorist they had stopped for a traffic violation, tempers again rose. When the police officers were found not guilty at their trial in 1992, Los Angeles again erupted in a damaging riot.

Demands for racial justice made California an important battleground in the civil rights movement. During the 1950s and '60s, older civil rights organizations like the NAACP joined with newer groups like the Congress of Racial Equality (CORE) to protest unfair hiring practices and segregation in California restaurants and department stores. In 1963, 30,000 people attended a civil rights rally in San Francisco.

California was the home to one of the most important protest groups of the 1960s and 1970s: the Black Panther Party. Bobby Seale and Huey P. Newton founded the Black Panthers in Oakland in 1966. They were influenced both by African American nationalist leaders like Malcolm X and by writers who urged poor people to fight back against a society that was unfair to them. The Black Panthers made news when they carried guns to the California state capitol to protest a law that would have banned openly carrying firearms. They argued that armed resistance was necessary to protect black people from a police force that could not be trusted. The Black Panthers' message of black power made them popular among some, but the FBI and Governor Ronald Reagan thought them a serious threat to public safety.

Pressure from the government, internal fighting, and some violent incidents led to the Black Panther Party losing support in the 1970s. However, the food, housing, and education programs they sponsored remained popular in Oakland and other cities. In 1977, members of the Black Panthers helped elect Lionel Wilson as Oakland's first African American mayor.

The Los Angeles entertainment industry brought the work of African American artists to the nation. Rap music of the 1980s and '90s expressed anger at the police and vividly depicted community suffering. In the film industry, African American writers and directors depicted Los Angeles in such movies as *Devil in a Blue Dress* and *Boyz N the Hood*. In 2000, the NAACP signed agreements with all four major television networks in which the networks promised to increase the ethnic diversity of the people who worked on television shows.

At the end of the 20th century, things were much different for African Americans in California than they had been one hundred years earlier. In 1900, only one California city had over 2,000 African Americans living there. By 1990, seven California cities had over 50,000 African Americans. In 1998, Los Angeles County was home to over one million black citizens.

African Americans have joined people of European, Latino, Asian, and Native heritage to make California the most diverse state in America.

ALLEN ALLENSWORTH

Town Founder

(1842-1914)

The year was 1912. In the town of Allensworth, located in Tulare County, lived 100 people. Many were farmers who grew such crops as cotton, sugar beets, and grain. They had a school, general stores, and several churches. There was also a debating society, a children's glee club, and a library.

The town of Allensworth was much like other small towns in California in the early 1900s. The difference was that all the people who lived there were African Americans.

Up from Slavery

Allen Allensworth was born April 7, 1842, in Louisville, Kentucky. Though born a slave, he quickly showed his determination to better his life. Allensworth learned to read and write even though it was difficult and dangerous for a slave to do so. This was discovered when Allen was 12, and he was punished by being sold away from his family. Allensworth remained a slave until he used the turmoil of the Civil War to get away and escape behind the lines of Union troops. Allensworth wanted to fight for freedom. In 1863, he joined the U.S. Navy and served until the end of the war.

The Colonel

When the war was over, Allensworth went to Roger Williams University in Tennessee to study religion. There he met his future wife, a teacher named Josephine Leavell. Allensworth became a minister and preached throughout the 1870s and beyond. He also became active in politics and served as a delegate to the Republican national conventions in 1880 and 1884.

In 1882, a black soldier asked Allensworth for his help in getting African American chaplains for black army units. Allensworth wrote to President Grover Cleveland asking to be appointed an army chaplain. In 1886, Allensworth became the only African American chaplain in the U.S. Army. For the next 20 years, he worked with black soldiers to educate them and assist them with spiritual matters. He retired as a lieutenant colonel, the army's highest-ranking black officer.

The "Colonel" spent the next several years lecturing to African Americans. In his speeches, Allensworth praised black educator Booker T. Washington's theories and his belief that blacks must be willing to help themselves. To do so, they should become better educated and learn job skills. In that way, Allensworth preached, blacks could be successful and convince whites to treat them better.

The Town of Allensworth

Allensworth met California teacher William Payne while on a lecture tour. The two men decided to create an all-black community in California that would reflect Booker T. Washington's theories about black self-help. In 1908, Allensworth and Payne acquired land from the Pacific Farming Company. The land was located in Tulare County, 30 miles north of Bakersfield. It seemed to be good farming land, which was important to Washington's teachings. Perhaps most importantly, the town was on a railroad line between Los Angeles and San Francisco. Their train station on the Santa Fe Railroad guaranteed business for the new community.

Allensworth worked hard to get the word out about the town, which was soon named after him. He advertised the town's farming opportunities and California's wonderful weather. He also tried to get black soldiers to make a home there.

The town was an immediate success. African Americans, both in Allensworth and elsewhere, were proud of this all-black community. Reporters from several African American newspapers wrote stories about the town. Delilah Beasley praised the town repeatedly in her book,

The Negro Trail Blazers of California, and forecast that it was "destined to be one of the great Negro cities in the United States."

The town's success, however, did not last long. Residents of Allensworth always felt that the Santa Fe Railroad Company discriminated against blacks. In 1914, the company built a new track and shifted its business away from Allensworth. It also turned out to be very expensive to supply the town with water and by the 1920s the water supply was beginning to run out. Most tragically, however, Allen Allensworth was killed in 1914 when a motorcycle struck him as he crossed a street. The town never recovered from the loss of its strongest leader.

Legacy

In the decades following Allensworth's death, the town named after him died as well. Still, he is remembered for his accomplishment of creating, even for a short time, a successful all-black town despite the obstacles faced by African Americans in the early 20th century.

In 1976, the town was named Colonel Allensworth State Historic Park. Today, we can visit the place where a determined former slave created a community to show what African Americans could accomplish.

Quote is from Bunche, Lonnie G., "Allensworth: The Life, Death, and Rebirth of an All-Black Community," *The Californians* 5 (1987): 26-33.

DELILAH BEASLEY

Journalist

(1866?-1934)

Early accounts of California made little mention of the contributions of African Americans. Delilah Beasley helped correct that problem. Through her writings, Beasley worked tirelessly to show the importance of blacks in California history and to show the contributions they made to society.

Early Life

Although we do not know all of the details of Delilah Leontium Beasley's early life, some of the facts are clear. Beasley grew up in Cincinnati, Ohio, and received some formal schooling there. Both of her parents died when she was young and the rest of her family was scattered. Obviously a bright child, Delilah had some of her writing published in a Cleveland newspaper when she was about 12 years old. By the time she was 15, she had written a column for the *Cincinnati Enquirer*.

To support herself, Beasley took a job as a maid with a wealthy family. She traveled with the family to Illinois and while there, began to study massage therapy. After working as a maid and masseuse in Ohio, she enrolled in a massage school in Buffalo, New York. She then moved to Michigan and became an instructor and massage therapist specializing in giving massages to pregnant women.

Beasley's life changed when she journeyed to Berkeley to work with a massage client. While in California, she learned of the many black communities around the state and became interested in the role of African Americans in California history. In about 1910, she returned to California determined to tell that story to the world.

Blazing Trails

Beasley spent the next decade traveling up and down the state of California. She lived in Berkeley, Oakland, and Los Angeles while she conducted research and wrote her book. Beasley spent time in libraries throughout the state reviewing old newspapers and documents. She also interviewed many people, including Annie Peters, an African American woman who had moved to California in 1851. Beasley consulted with historians, reporters, and writers when preparing her book.

In 1919, *The Negro Trail-Blazers of California* was published. Beasley's book was filled with over 300 pages of information and a great number of pictures and illustrations. Beasley's goal, according to one writer who has studied her, "was nothing less than to recast California history by including in it virtually every instance of participation and contribution by Black Americans." Indeed, the book was the first of its kind. Beasley realized that no one had written a history book that focused on African Americans in California. Moreover, most histories of California largely ignored blacks' contributions.

Beasley's History

Beasley's book covered all parts of California history. She showed that there were a number of Africans who explored California with the Spanish during the 16th century. She also showed that blacks were involved in the Spanish Empire in Mexico and that many entered California from the south. She noted, as historians now agree, that many of the founders of the city of Los Angeles were of African descent. The early picture of California as one of Europeans and natives, therefore, was incomplete.

Beasley also showed how slavery affected California's development. Even though California was officially a "free state" that did not allow slavery, Beasley demonstrated that many slaves lived and worked in California. *Negro Trail-Blazers* includes descriptions of the lives of African Americans who were illegally held in slavery in California. The book also shows the African Americans, like San Francisco businesswoman and activist Mary Ellen Pleasant, who devoted their time and energy to fighting slavery.

Negro Trail-Blazers tells of what happened in California after the Civil War. Beasley details African Americans' fight for public education for their children. The book also touches on such issues as the gold rush, the growth of churches, and the development of civil rights organizations in the state.

The book's focus on biographies, the telling of people's lives, was seen both as one of the book's greatest strengths and also one of its worst problems. Beasley, who had no formal historical training, saw her work as something that could appeal to everyone. She told stories of African American heroes that were meant to inspire people. She hoped that African Americans would be made proud by these stories and that whites would receive an important education.

Some people, however, criticized the book because of this focus on African American heroes. They pointed out, accurately, that Beasley said only good things about the African Americans she profiled. While the book had many important insights, critics felt that Beasley's desire to praise African Americans overcame her good judgment. Despite these criticisms, *Negro Trail-Blazers* was soon in libraries throughout California and beyond.

Journalist

The success of *Negro Trail-Blazers* in California helped Beasley's career as a journalist. While she wrote her book, she contributed articles to the *Oakland Sunshine* and the *Oakland Tribune*. In 1923, Delilah Beasley became the first African American woman in California to have a regular newspaper column. Until her death in 1934, Beasley regularly wrote a column called "Activities Among Negroes" for the *Oakland Tribune*.

Beasley had important goals for her newspaper work. "The one object" of her column, Beasley wrote, "has always been to create a better understanding between races." Beasley's columns focused on issues like the importance of education and the need for racial harmony.

As the name of the column implies, Beasley wrote about African Americans and their lives. She gave brief biographies of people and told of events, like weddings, that occurred in African American communities throughout the state and the country.

Beasley was much more than a well-intentioned gossip columnist. She was also a strong fighter for civil and human rights. She belonged to a number of social and political organizations, including the National Association for the Advancement of Colored People (NAACP). She often used her columns to tell about these organizations and their work.

Shortly after she began writing her column, one incident helped bring her national attention. Beasley went to the International Convention of Women in Washington, D.C. While there, she reported that the American Music House had refused to allow African Americans to participate in a prominent concert. Some reporters used offensive language to refer to the African Americans. Beasley organized a meeting of the journalists in Washington and explained to them why such language should not be used. She had some success in getting newspapers to use the term "Negro," to refer to Americans of African descent.

Delilah Beasley died of heart disease in August 1934. She had never married and had no close relatives.

Legacy

Delilah Beasley devoted her life to educating whites and blacks alike about African American experiences in California. Her book, *The Negro Trail-Blazers in California*, was an important milestone in the telling of California history. Never again would writers be able to claim that African Americans were not important in the history of the state. Beasley, like many of the people, about whom she wrote, was a true trailblazer.

Quotes are from Crouchett, Lorraine J. *Delilah Leontium Beasley: Oakland's Crusading Journalist*. Downey Place Publishing, 1990.

RALPH BUNCHE

Diplomat

(1903*-1971)

Ralph Bunche, the first African American to be awarded a Nobel Peace Prize, was an American diplomat whose commitment to freedom made him a respected figure throughout the world.

Growing Up

Ralph Johnson Bunche was born in Detroit, Michigan, on August 7, 1903. His father, Fred, was a barber from Kansas. Olive, Bunche's mother, had both white and black ancestors, including an Irish planter and a black slave. As a child, Bunche lived in a variety of places, including Ohio, Tennessee, and New Mexico. Music was important in his household and, though they were poor, Bunche considered his childhood a happy one.

Everything changed for Bunche when he was 13 years old. In 1917, his mother died of tuberculosis and his uncle committed suicide. Fred, who had left the family to seek work, did not come back and never saw his son

*Reports of a 1904 birth date are based on an incorrect duplicate birth certificate.

again. From then on, Ralph's grandmother, Lucy Johnson, took care of Ralph and his sister. In an effort to give the family a new start, she added the "e" to the Bunche name and took the family to Los Angeles.

The Central Avenue area in Los Angeles, where the family moved in 1918, was mostly white but home to a growing number of African Americans. "Nana" Johnson was a strict Baptist with a lot of racial pride. Although she could have "passed" as a white person, she refused to do so. Ralph, who was also light-skinned, would take his grandmother's teachings to heart.

Ralph was an excellent student. After graduating at the top of his high school class, he entered college at UCLA. There he played on the football and basketball teams, wrote for the college newspaper and, when excluded from the debating society because of his race, formed another debating group. When he graduated in 1927, he was again at the top of his class. In his graduation speech, the political science major talked about the importance of being a "socially valuable man." Bunche would devote the rest of his life to that cause.

Scholar

Bunche went from UCLA to Harvard, where he earned his M. A. degree in political science. He then took a job at Howard University, a prestigious school primarily serving African Americans. In addition to his success as a popular teacher and administrator at Howard, Bunche found happiness there as well. In 1930, shortly after he had returned to Harvard to begin studying for his Ph.D. degree, Bunche married Ruth Ethel Harris, a former student of his at Howard. Bunche completed his Ph.D. degree in government and international relations in 1934, winning a prize for his work at Harvard.

Over the next decade, Bunche became one of the nation's most respected scholars. In addition to his work on Africa, he became an expert on racial issues in the U.S. Working with Gunnar Myrdal, a Swedish professor, he helped write the influential *An American Dilemma: The Negro Problem and Modern Democracy* in 1944.

Diplomat

During World War II, Bunche was an analyst for the United States government. He worked to increase the role of African Americans in the war effort and wrote the manual given to U.S. troops who served in Africa. After the war, Bunche served in the State Department. He was one of the leading American diplomats helping to create the United Nations charter.

In 1946, Bunche left U.S. government service and went to work for the United Nations. He was in charge of the Trusteeship department, which had responsibility for over 14 million people living in places that had once been colonies of other countries. The United Nations was helping them become fully independent countries. In 1948, Bunche was called on to help the UN mediator end the war between the new state of Israel and its Arab neighbors. When the mediator was assassinated in 1949, Bunche was promoted to take this difficult and dangerous role. Dealing first with Israel's conflict with Egypt, and later with Jordan, Syria, and Lebanon, Bunche managed to bring about the end of the Arab-Israeli War.

The following year, Ralph Bunche became the first African American to win the Nobel Peace Prize. At first Bunche wanted to refuse the honor because he believed that "peacemaking at the UN was not done for prizes." Bunche had a long and distinguished career at the United Nations, where he continued his work until shortly before his death from diabetes-related illnesses in 1971.

Legacy

By the time of Bunche's death, he was one of the most honored people of the nation. In addition to his Nobel Peace Prize, he received the U.S. Medal of Freedom, the Presidential Medal of Honor, and the NAACP's Spingarn Medal. Many universities gave him honorary degrees and his old school, UCLA, named a building in his honor. The awards pay tribute to a man who dedicated his life to peace, freedom, and international cooperation.

Quotes are from Urquhart, Brian. *Ralph Bunche: An American Life*. Norton, 1993.

JACKIE ROBINSON

Athlete

(1919-1972)

Jackie Robinson was one of the best baseball players of all time. By breaking the "color line" that kept African Americans out of Major League Baseball, Robinson also became one of the great civil rights heroes of the 20th century.

Baseball's all-time leading home run hitter, Hank Aaron, has called him the "Dr. King of baseball." But perhaps the most important testimony to Robinson's importance came from Martin Luther King, Jr. himself. Said Dr. King, "without [Jackie Robinson], I would never have been able to do what I did."

Growing Up

Jack Roosevelt Robinson was born in Cairo, Georgia, in 1919. Robinson's father, Jerry, was a sharecropper who left soon after Jackie's birth. The Robinson family, like that of many African Americans, decided that it was time to leave the South. Mallie, Jackie's mother, took Jackie and his four brothers and sisters out of Georgia and moved to Pasadena, California.

Pasadena was a mostly white community. Despite community resistance when the Robinson family moved into a white neighborhood, Jackie and his brothers and sister grew up in an interracial environment.

Just because blacks and whites lived together, however, does not mean that they always got along. As a child, Jackie frequently dealt with people who made fun of him because of his race. Jackie did not take these insults lightly. He was quick-tempered and got into more than his share of fights.

Jackie was happiest when he played sports, and he excelled in almost all of them. The star athlete found that his success made his teammates friendlier to him. Jackie also had an excellent role model. His older brother Mack finished second to Jesse Owens in the 200-meter dash during the 1936 Olympic games. By the time he had finished high school, Jackie had become a successful athlete in several major sports.

After attending Pasadena Junior College for two years, Robinson transferred to UCLA, where he starred in several sports. He led the conference in scoring as a basketball player and almost took his team to the Rose Bowl as a running back in football. He also set a national college record in the broad jump. Baseball, in which he would become famous, was considered his worst sport.

Soldier and Ballplayer

Driven by a desire to make money, Jackie Robinson left UCLA in 1941 before earning his degree. He worked briefly for the National Youth Administration, a New Deal program in which he tutored young people to play sports. He also played semi-pro football and basketball during this time.

Shortly after the United States entered World War II, Robinson was drafted. He applied to Officers' Candidate School (OCS). Despite his skill as a rifleman, his education, and his obvious intelligence, he was turned down because of his race. After Robinson enlisted the help of African American heavyweight boxing champion Joe Louis, the army reconsidered. Robinson graduated from OCS in January 1943 as a second lieutenant.

Robinson complained about the segregation and the poor treatment that blacks received while serving their country. He was often in trouble with higher-ranking officers who did not share Robinson's views on race.

While serving in Texas, Jackie Robinson got in trouble for refusing to sit at the back of a bus, years before Rosa Parks would become famous for doing the same thing. When the white bus driver became hostile at the refusal of his orders, Jackie shouted right back at him. Military officers took Robinson into custody. He was charged with insubordination, showing disrespect to a superior officer (after he was arrested), and public drunkenness (even though he did not drink). Robinson was found not guilty in a court-martial hearing, and was soon given a medical discharge and sent on his way.

In 1945, Jackie Robinson joined the Kansas City Monarchs of the Negro Leagues. The Negro Leagues had formed because Major League Baseball refused to admit African Americans. Negro League baseball had many fans throughout the nation. Teams of Negro League all-stars often beat teams of Major League all-stars when they played in exhibition games.

Robinson played shortstop for the Monarchs, learning from great players like Satchel Paige, Buck O'Neill, and Cool Papa Bell. Although his skills improved, Robinson did not enjoy the low pay and poor conditions that were part of Negro League life.

Major Leagues

For decades, a "gentlemen's agreement" among baseball owners ensured that African Americans were kept out of Major League Baseball. Branch Rickey, the owner of the Brooklyn Dodgers, was determined to change this policy. Rickey searched not only for a great ballplayer, but also for a person who had the character and temperament to deal with the trials of being the only black player in the Major Leagues. In 1945, Branch Rickey met with Jackie Robinson and told him that he needed him to have the "courage" not to fight back, even if things became rough. Robinson agreed that, no matter what the insult, he would remain silent.

1946 was an important year for Jackie Robinson. In February he married his college sweetheart Rachel Isum. Soon after, he began playing for the Dodgers farm team in Montreal, Canada. Robinson played well that year and earned the friendship of his teammates and the admiration of the fans. Nevertheless, opposing players used rough play and insults to upset him. By the end of the season, he was suffering from nervous exhaustion.

In 1947, Jackie Robinson went to spring training with the Dodgers. Training that year was moved from Florida to Cuba so that Robinson would not have to live in the hostile South. A number of Dodgers players, especially ones who had grown up in the segregated South, did not want to play with Robinson. There was even talk of a players' strike. The Dodgers however were firm. By the end of the spring training, Jackie Robinson was a full-fledged member of the Brooklyn Dodgers.

Jackie Robinson's participation in baseball made him one of the most loved and hated ballplayers ever to take the field. Opposing players, coaches, and fans showered him with insults and offensive racial attacks. Pitchers routinely threw the ball at him and opposing players drove their metal spikes into his leg. When he traveled with the team, Robinson could not stay in the same hotel and often could not eat with his teammates. Even so, Robinson knew that the whole world was watching him and that he could not complain.

Despite all that he had to endure, this "experiment" was a great success. Black newspapers throughout the nation followed the Robinson story with interest. The Dodgers' attendance boomed as Robinson's celebrity brought thousands of new fans to the ballpark. Robinson became a valued friend to many of his teammates and his good relationship with them, especially with Southern-born Pee Wee Reese, gradually won Robinson acceptance.

Robinson had success on the field. He hit .297 and led the National League in stolen bases. He soon became known for his daring and aggressive running style. Robinson won the 1947 Rookie of the Year award (the award is now named after him) and helped lead his team to the National League pennant.

For the next decade, Robinson was one of the game's best players. By 1949, he was free to talk back to opponents. No longer worried that one wrong move could set back African Americans for decades to come, Robinson had his finest season. Playing second base, he led the National League with a .342 batting average, stole 37 bases (the best in the majors), and won the Most Valuable Player award. Robinson also played himself in a movie about his life.

Robinson's success paved the way for other African American ballplayers in the Major Leagues. By 1959, every team had at least one black player.

By that time, however, Robinson was not one of those players. In 1955, he had helped lead the Dodgers to a World Series victory over the New York Yankees. But by 1957, he had had enough. Injuries and diabetes had taken their toll and robbed Robinson of much of his ability. Rather than accept a trade to the rival New York Giants, Robinson retired.

Life after Baseball

Jackie Robinson continued to be outspoken about civil rights issues after his playing days were over. He wrote a column in the *New York Post* and later a column in the major black newspaper of the era, the *Amsterdam News*. He became an officer in the NAACP, a group which years earlier had honored him with their Spingarn Medal. Robinson used his fame to support a young minister with whom he had become friends, Dr. Martin Luther King, Jr.

Robinson also went into politics. He supported Richard Nixon's 1960 presidential campaign, although he later came to regret that support, and worked as an aide to New York governor Nelson Rockefeller. Robinson was often criticized for his political positions. Younger, more radical, black activists accused him of being an "Uncle Tom" for his close associations with whites. Robinson even got into a much-publicized newspaper debate with Malcolm X.

Nevertheless, Robinson continued to speak out for causes important to the black community. He raised money for Martin Luther King, Jr.'s campaign to rebuild Southern churches and helped found a bank to serve the people of Harlem. In a celebration honoring him at the 1972 World Series, shortly before his death, he pointed out that baseball still had no black managers.

Legacy

Jackie Robinson was elected to the Baseball Hall of Fame in 1962. In 1997, Major League Baseball permanently retired his uniform number 42, the only player ever so honored.

But Robinson's skills on the field, great as they were, were not nearly as important as what he accomplished for African Americans, and all Americans, by playing. Perhaps no single event in the civil rights movement had a greater effect on the hearts and minds of Americans. Robinson once said that "a life is not important except in the impact it has on other lives." By that standard, Jackie Robinson's life was one of the most important in all of American history.

Quotes on page 33 are from Falkner, David. *Great Time Coming.* Simon & Schuster, 1995; quote on page 40 is from Ward, Geoffrey C. and Ken Burns. *Baseball: An Illustrated History.* Knopf, 1994.

THOMAS BRADLEY

Mayor

(1917 - 1998)

Thomas Bradley, a grandson of slaves, rose from humble beginnings to become the popular leader of the second largest city in the nation.

Tom Bradley was born in Calvert, Texas, on December 29, 1917. His parents, Lee and Crenner Bradley, were sharecroppers. When Tom was three, the family moved to Dallas and, by 1924, traveled by car to Arizona.

Growing up in Los Angeles

From Arizona, Tom's father Lee went to Los Angeles in search of work. Although jobs were difficult to find, Lee became a porter on the Santa Fe Railroad. By the end of 1924, Crenner and the children joined Lee and settled in the East Side of Los Angeles.

The Bradley family story was hardly unique. At this time in history, many African Americans were leaving the South. Improved transportation and the possibility of better jobs in northern cities encouraged many blacks to leave the area in which their ancestors had lived as slaves. Many Americans of all races and backgrounds were looking for new opportunities in the West.

As the second child, Bradley became an important member of his household, particularly after his parents divorced. Bradley earned money for the family with a paper route and helped his mother, who worked as a maid, when she cleaned houses. Tom also took care of the younger children.

"While others were out playing ball I would often slip into my seat during recess and read a book," Bradley once recalled. By the time he was ready for high school, Bradley knew that education could be his ticket to success. Using the address of one of his mother's friendly clients and with the help of the school's track coach, Bradley was able to enroll at Polytechnic High School, a mostly white school with a far better reputation than the high school in Tom's neighborhood.

Bradley thrived at "Poly." He became a student leader and a star member of the track and football teams. He was sometimes asked to solve problems between students, especially racial disputes. In his first campaign victory, Bradley was elected president of the Poly Boys' League, a major accomplishment in a school in which blacks were not allowed to join many student clubs.

Bradley's Rise

Bradley enrolled at UCLA in 1937 with a full athletic scholarship. Although he was a good student, Bradley left college after he scored well on the entrance exam for the Los Angeles police academy. Looking for the financial stability that he knew a police job could provide, Bradley joined the LAPD.

Bradley had to fight racism, both inside and outside the police force. He often received inferior job assignments because of his race. This was perhaps not surprising in a force that still had segregated police cars. Nevertheless, Bradley compiled an excellent record and rose through the ranks as a policeman. As a lieutenant, he became the LAPD's highest-ranking African American officer.

Bradley wanted more than just a police career. In 1941, he married Ethel Arnold, a longtime friend from church. The couple had two children, Lorraine and Phyllis. Bradley took law classes at night and became an attorney. In 1956, the Bradleys moved to a new house in the mostly white Crenshaw section of Los Angeles. By 1961, Bradley retired from the police force to concentrate on his law practice.

Political Career

In 1962, Bradley was one of a number of local political leaders who met with Dr. Martin Luther King, Jr. to discuss ways to elect a black councilman to represent Los

Angeles's 10th district. The following year, Bradley entered the race.

The 10th district was racially mixed with a sizable white majority and many Jewish voters. Bradley's friendly manner and his history as a policeman, lawyer, and community activist made him a strong candidate. Unlike many African American politicians in the era, Bradley combined his ability to win black votes with popularity among white voters (particularly Jewish ones). He soundly defeated his Republican opponent and became the first African American elected to the Los Angeles city council.

Races for Mayor

In 1969, Bradley decided to challenge the mayor, Sam Yorty, in the next election. Bradley's campaign was particularly exciting for his many black supporters. But Bradley also had support in white, Latino, and Asian communities. Though Bradley did better than any African American had ever done in any election in a major American city, Yorty defeated Bradley in the race.

Four years later, Bradley ran again. The councilman, who had been elected to his third term in 1971, was now a well-known Los Angeles figure. Bradley ran an effective campaign and won with 54 percent of the vote. The nation's third-largest city now had an African American mayor.

The Mayor

Over the next twenty years, Tom Bradley became one of the most popular officials in the history of Los Angeles. As mayor, he dedicated himself to two goals: city growth and racial healing. Under his leadership, Los Angeles grew richer, and passed Chicago as the city with the second-most people in the country (after New York).

Bradley wanted more than wealth for the city; he also wanted its people to live in harmony. He brought people of all races, both men and women, into his administration and worked tirelessly to promote good racial relations. Personally, the tall, dignified man became a well-liked ambassador for the city.

Perhaps Bradley's greatest success came in 1984 when Los Angeles hosted the Olympic Games. There is a financial risk to having the Olympics. Bradley, who had witnessed some of the 1932 Los Angeles Olympics as a child, made a good deal with the International Olympic Committee. Under his leadership, the 1984 Olympics were a huge financial success and brought great publicity to Los Angeles.

Setbacks

In 1982, Tom Bradley ran for governor of California. After winning the Democratic primary, Bradley faced state Attorney General George Deukmejian in a tough campaign. Although most public opinion polls said

Bradley was likely to win, vote returns on Election Day showed him 93,000 votes short (out of almost 8,000,000 cast) of being the first African American elected governor of any state in the union.

Bradley ran for governor again in 1986 but lost badly. His political career, however, was not over. In 1989, Bradley won an amazing fifth term as mayor. Those last four years were the toughest for Bradley. A financial scandal harmed his popularity. More tragically, the police beating of a black motorist, Rodney King, led to riots after a white jury acquitted the police officers. Both the verdict and the riots saddened the man who had dedicated so much of his career to racial understanding.

Legacy

Tom Bradley was an important figure in the history of California and the nation. As the mayor of Los Angeles, he proved that an African American could become an effective and popular leader of a large and diverse city.

After his fifth term as mayor, Bradley once again took up his law career. He died in 1998 after a second heart attack. At his funeral, religious leaders, entertainers, celebrities, and statesmen paid tribute to a quiet, studious man who became one of the most important political leaders in California history.

Quote is from Payne, J. Gregory and Scott C. Ratzan. *Tom Bradley: The Impossible Dream*. Roundtable Publishing, 1986.

FLORENCE GRIFFITH JOYNER

Athlete

(1959 - 1998)

She was called "the fastest woman in the world." Yet Florence Griffith Joyner may be best remembered for her glittering 6-inch fingernails and her designer running clothes. "FloJo," as she came to be known, became an American hero after her success in the 1988 Olympic Games.

Dee Dee

Delorez Florence Griffith was born in Los Angeles on December 21, 1959. The seventh of 11 children, Delorez, nicknamed "Dee Dee," grew up in public housing projects in Watts. Dee Dee's parents divorced in 1963. Two years later, the mostly black Watts neighborhood erupted in rioting that stunned the nation and further devastated the community.

Dee Dee became an athlete at an early age. She started running track as a seven-year old, in part because the sport was free and required no expensive equipment.

Sports were not her only interest, however. She learned a number of skills from her family, including knitting, crocheting, and braiding hair. She also had her own sense of style. Dee Dee was known for wearing mismatched socks. She mixed crayon with her mother's nail polish in order to make more interesting colors. When a teacher once asked her what she intended to be, the girl responded "Everything. I want to be everything." Although it was a strange answer, the teacher may not have wanted to argue with a child who wore mismatched socks and had a boa constrictor for a pet.

Florence Griffith

Griffith was a successful athlete all through school. In 1974 and 1975, she earned trips to the Jesse Owens National Youth Games in San Francisco. There she met Owens, the great African American track star whose success in the 1936 Olympics humiliated Adolf Hitler.

Griffith attended California State University at Northridge (CSUN), where she was tutored by top track coach Bob Kersee. While a good runner, Griffith never became a star in college. After transferring, she graduated from UCLA in 1983.

The following year, Florence Griffith made the Olympic team and was able to participate in the 1984 Olympic Games in her home city of Los Angeles. At the Olympics, Griffith won a silver medal in the 200-meter dash.

After the Olympics, Griffith began working at a bank during the days and braiding hair at nights, even though she was one of the top female sprinters in the world. By 1987, however, her outlook changed. In that year, she married Al Joyner. Joyner was an Olympic triple jump champion and the brother of Jackie Joyner-Kersee, perhaps the finest female athlete in the world. Jackie Joyner-Kersee was married to Bob Kersee, Florence's old track coach. In 1988, Florence once again enlisted Bob Kersee to coach her.

FloJo

Florence Griffith Joyner burst onto the American scene in the 1988 Olympic trials. Sporting long, painted fingernails and wearing a skintight "athletic negligee" that left one leg exposed, Griffith Joyner shattered the world record in the hundred meters. Suddenly, "FloJo" was a household word.

FloJo's performance in the 1988 Olympics in Seoul, South Korea, was one of the great individual athletic feats in the century. She set an Olympic record in the 100 meters, a world record in the 200 meters, and won her third gold medal in the 400-meter relay. She also won a silver medal in the 1600 meters. FloJo became an American hero. That year, she won the Sullivan award given to the nation's best amateur athlete and the Associated Press's Female Athlete of the Year award.

Only unproven rumors that her success was due to illegal performance-enhancing drugs tarnished her great year.

FloJo devoted much of the rest of her short life to helping charitable causes. She also served as a co-chair of the President's Counsel on Physical Fitness. In 1998, Griffith Joyner suffered a heart attack and seizure and died. She was just 38 years old.

Legacy

Florence Griffith Joyner's athletic accomplishments were impressive. She was the first American woman to win four track and field medals at an Olympic Games. At the time of her death (and as of January 2000), she still held the world records in the 100 and 200 meters. So great were her talents that the person who became known as "the fastest woman in the world" was recently named the 11th best female athlete of the 20th century by *Sports Illustrated for Women.*

But for those who saw her run, she will not be remembered simply as Griffith Joyner, Olympic athlete. For them, she will always be FloJo, a woman whose style and talent made her a figure larger than life.

Quote on page 48 is from *The Los Angeles Times*, September 22, 1998.

WALTER MOSLEY

Author

(1952 -   )

Walter Mosley was born on January 12, 1952, and grew up in Watts, a mainly black part of Los Angeles. Although he is generally thought of exclusively as an African American writer, his ethnic heritage is actually more diverse. His father, Leroy, was an African American from Louisiana. His mother, Ella, was of white, Jewish ancestry and was from New York. Both parents' families were great storytellers, and told tales of living in the American South and, in the case of his mother, in Eastern Europe. Mosley later pointed to his father's storytelling, more than any books he had read, as what influenced him to become a writer.

Writer

Mosley grew up somewhat poor but, after graduating high school, was able to attend college in Vermont. His bad work habits led to him transferring schools but he eventually graduated college with a degree in political science. After briefly studying political science at the

University of Massachusetts, Mosley worked at a variety of jobs, including catering, selling pottery, and computer programming.

By 1985, Mosley decided to focus on his writing. He entered a graduate program in writing at the City College of New York (CCNY) and began creating the character of Easy Rawlins. Mosley was not an immediate success. His first book, *Gone Fishin'*, was rejected by many publishers and agents. His big break came in 1989 when he showed his new Easy Rawlins book, *Devil in a Blue Dress*, to his professor at CCNY. Within two months, his book had been bought by one of the largest publishers in the United States. All of a sudden, Walter Mosley became a popular and respected author.

Easy Rawlins

Devil in a Blue Dress is a mystery novel set in Los Angeles after World War II. Many mystery writers, like Dashiell Hammett and Raymond Chandler, had become famous writing stories about tough detectives and their work in cities like San Francisco and Los Angeles. Mosley's book was instantly compared to the work of those great writers. There was one major difference, however; Mosley's hero was black.

Easy Rawlins is introduced in the book as a World War II veteran who loses his job at an aircraft factory because of racism. When approached by a white man to search for a white woman who was known to go to jazz clubs in African American neighborhoods, Rawlins, somewhat accidentally, begins his career as a private detective.

Devil in a Blue Dress and the other Easy Rawlins books that have followed it use detail to describe life in African American communities of Los Angeles in the 1940s, 1950s, and 1960s. As the books progress, Rawlins deals with racism, financial troubles, and family turmoil. At the same time, Mosley vividly shows what society was like in Rawlins' corner of the world.

Devil in a Blue Dress earned Walter Mosley great recognition. The book was nominated for an Edgar award, the highest honor given to a mystery book in America. When presidential candidate Bill Clinton praised the novel, the book became even more popular. In 1995, *Devil in a Blue Dress* was made into a movie starring Denzel Washington as Easy Rawlins.

Other Work

Although he is best known for the six Easy Rawlins novels, Mosley has also received praise for his other work. Two of his books are set in modern-day Watts and center on African American philosopher and ex-convict Socrates Fortlow. *Always Outnumbered, Always Outgunned*, the first of these Socrates Fortlow books, was made into an HBO movie starring Laurence Fishburne. Mosley recently published his first science fiction novel, *Blue Light*, which is set in the San Francisco Bay Area during the 1960s. In addition, he is an award-winning short story author and a past president of the Mystery Writers of America.

Community Involvement

As Mosley has become more successful in his career, he has devoted himself to improving and publicizing African Americans' success in the arts and society. When he published his novel *Gone Fishin'* in 1987, he chose to work with Black Classic Press, which is run by African Americans. At New York University, he created a popular lecture series on "Black Genius." During these lectures, successful African Americans from all fields speak to students and the university community.

Legacy

When the 1990s began, few people had heard of Walter Mosley. Ten years later, this storyteller's books have been translated into 20 languages and Mosley has become a best-selling author who has won awards and dined at the White House. As a novelist, mystery writer, and science fiction author, Mosley focuses much of his attention on African American life in California. As a new decade begins, it seems certain that readers will be hearing more from Walter Mosley.

OTHER NOTABLE
AFRICAN AMERICANS
IN CALIFORNIA

James P. Beckwourth (1798?-1866?) – Mountain man who trapped beaver and explored in the West. He discovered Beckwourth Pass through the Sierra Nevada. The town of Beckwourth is named for him.

Willie L. Brown, Jr. (1934-   ) – California-educated attorney who served as a member of the California State Assembly from 1965 to 1995. An influential Speaker of the Assembly for 16 years, Brown was elected mayor of San Francisco in 1995.

Tony Gwynn (1960-   ) – Star outfielder with the San Diego Padres baseball team. Gwynn was born and raised in Southern California. He joined the Padres in 1982 and went on to win a string of batting titles.

Augustus F. Hawkins (1907-   ) – Congressman from Los Angeles serving from 1963 to 1991 in the U.S. House of Representatives as the first black Representative from west of the Rockies. Before this, he was a California State Assemblyman (1935-62), where he introduced and helped to pass California's Fair Employment Practices Act of 1959.

Rafer Johnson (1935-   ) – Olympic medal winner in the decathlon in 1956 and 1960. Johnson set a world record in the decathlon as a college student at UCLA. In 1960 he won the Sullivan Award as the outstanding U.S. amateur athlete.

Sargent Claude Johnson (1887-1967) – Sculptor and printmaker, Johnson served as West Coast director of the Works Progress Administration. His sculptures depicting African Americans are in a number of San Francisco buildings as well as in New York art galleries.

William A. Leidesdorff (1810-1848) – Wealthy landowner who came to San Francisco in 1841 as the captain of a trading ship, and stayed as a merchant and city official. He acquired several large land grants from the government, including the area around Leidesdorff Street in San Francisco.

Biddy Mason (1818-1891) – Brought to Southern California in 1851 as a slave, she won her freedom through the courts. Her skills as a midwife and herbalist enabled her to become a prosperous property owner in Los Angeles.

Terry McMillan (1951-   ) – Author of popular novels about life among black Americans today. McMillan came to California at the age of 17. She is best known for *Waiting to Exhale* (1992) and *How Stella Got Her Groove Back* (1996), both of which have been made into movies.

Mary Ellen Pleasant (1814?-1904) – Crusader for equal rights for African Americans in early California. Pleasant came to San Francisco in 1852, where she owned and operated boarding houses. Her business brought her contacts with many influential people.

Norma Sklarek (1928-   ) – First black woman to be licensed as an architect in the U.S., in 1954 in New York. Now part of a woman-owned architectural firm in Los Angeles, she designed Terminal One at the L.A. International Airport and the U.S. Embassy in Tokyo.

Morrie Turner (1923-   ) – Cartoonist and author of *Wee Pals*. A native of Oakland, Turner began drawing cartoons when he was in the 5th grade. He began the *Wee Pals* comic strip in 1965 to portray a world without prejudice.

Maxine Waters (1938-   ) – First black Congresswoman from California. Waters served as a member of the California Assembly from 1977-91. She became a Representative to the U.S. Congress in 1991, where she is now serving her fifth term.

Tiger Woods (1975-   ) – Golfer who, in 1997 at age 21, became the first African American and the youngest winner of the Masters Tournament. Born Eldrick Thon Woods in Cypress, California, Tiger learned golf as an infant from his father. He left Stanford University in 1996 to become a professional golfer.

INTERESTING FACTS AND FIGURES

Statistics

- People of African descent make up 12.7% of the United States population, according to U.S. Bureau of the Census estimates of July 1998. 34,430,569 African Americans live in the United States.

- California has 12.1% of the total U.S. population, and 7.13% of the nation's black population.

- 2,455,570 African Americans live in California. The only state with more African Americans than California is New York, with 3,219,676.

- 7.5% of California's population is black.

- California counties with the highest percentage of black residents are: Alameda County, 19.0%; Solano County, 14.0%; Los Angeles County, 11.3%; San Francisco County, 10.7%.

- Of the 2,455,570 black people in California, over 42% live in Los Angeles County (1,039,243).

Kwanzaa (KWAHN zuh)

Kwanzaa is a seven-day celebration that starts on December 26. This African American holiday began in the U.S. in 1966. It was developed and promoted by Dr. Maulana Karenga, a black cultural leader and professor of Pan-African studies at the University of California, Long Beach.

The word *Kwanzaa* is a Swahili (an East African language) word meaning *first fruits*. The holiday is based on the traditional African festival celebrating the first harvest of the crops. It includes a community feast, *karamu*, with African foods, music, and dancing. Each evening, family members light one of seven candles in a *kinara* (candleholder).

Martin Luther King, Jr. Day

Each year on the third Monday of January, people in the U.S. honor civil rights leader Dr. Martin Luther King, Jr. Many offices and schools are closed on this day as people take part in religious services, candlelight vigils, or parades honoring Dr. King, whose birthday was January 15, 1929. The plan to establish this federal holiday began in April 1968, just four days after Dr. King was assassinated. Over 15 years later, in November 1983, President Reagan signed the bill creating the holiday. It was first observed on January 20, 1986. By June 1999, all 50 states had adopted the holiday.

Soul Food

Soul food is the name given to a creative type of cooking that grew out of the black slave experience. African American slaves were given the food that their masters did not consider good enough to eat themselves. This included things like pig knuckles, ears, intestines, leftover beans, and the end of the corn. From these rejected scraps, slaves made meals for their families, adding wild greens, game such as squirrel and possum, and fish. Today, soul food is popular across the country in homes and restaurants. Favorite dishes are barbecued ribs, black-eyed peas, fried chitterlings (pig intestines), catfish, collard greens with hamhocks, cornbread, "dirty" rice, and mustard greens.

TIMELINE OF
AFRICAN AMERICANS
IN CALIFORNIA

1769   People of African descent are part of Spanish expedition from Mexico to *Alta California*.

1781   26 of the 46 people who establish Los Angeles have some African heritage.

1821   Mexico becomes independent from Spain.

1848   James Marshall's discovery of gold at Coloma triggers a gold rush that brings people of all races into California.

1850   California enters the union as a free (no slavery) state.

1855   First of four California Colored Conventions held to advocate for black civil rights.

1857   *Dred Scott* decision by U.S. Supreme Court rules that slaves do not become free by being in a free state, leading to fears of slavery spreading throughout the United States.

1861-65   United States fights a Civil War.

1865   Thirteenth Amendment to the United States Constitution outlaws slavery.

1868   Fourteenth Amendment to the United States Constitution guarantees legal and civil rights to all citizens regardless of race.

1870	Fifteenth Amendment to the United States Constitution guarantees right to vote to all male citizens regardless of race.
1906	Earthquake and fire devastate San Francisco, hastening African Americans move to suburbs like Oakland and Berkeley.
1908	The all-black town of Allensworth is founded.
1919	Delilah Beasley publishes *The Negro Trail-Blazers of California*.
1910s-1920s	African Americans leave the South for northern cities during the Great Migration. Some move to California.
1941	President Franklin D. Roosevelt signs Executive Order 8802. The law creates the Fair Employment Practices Committee to ensure equal treatment of African Americans in government hiring.
1941-45	World War II leads to African American migration to California.
1944	African American sailors protest working conditions after an explosion kills over 300 people at the Port Chicago Navy Base, east of San Francisco. Many are arrested and court-martialed.
1947	Jackie Robinson breaks color barrier when he joins the Brooklyn Dodgers.
1950	Ralph Bunche wins Nobel Peace Prize, the first African American so honored.

1962	Augustus Hawkins elected California's first African American congressman.
1965	Watts Riots shock Los Angeles and the nation.
1965	Maulana Ron Karenga creates Kwanzaa. Los Angeles-based Karenga becomes a leading spokesperson for black nationalism.
1966	Bobby Seale and Huey P. Newton found the Black Panther Party in Oakland.
1968	Tommie Smith and John Carlos, two runners from San Jose State University, give black power salute (raised clenched fist) while being honored at Olympic Games. Their medals were taken away for this action.
1972	Yvonne Braithwaite Burke elected California's first African American congresswoman.
1973	Tom Bradley elected first African American mayor of Los Angeles.
1980	Willie Brown elected speaker of the California Assembly.
1992	Rodney King riots occur in Los Angeles.
1996	California voters pass Proposition 209, ending affirmative action programs in the state.

FOR MORE INFORMATION ON AFRICAN AMERICANS IN CALIFORNIA

Books

Appiah, Kwame Anthony and Henry Louis Gates, Jr. *Africana: The Encyclopedia of the African and African American Experience.* Basic Books, 1999. (New, comprehensive and accurate adult-level reference source; also web site: *http://africana.com*)

Bergman, Irwin B. *Jackie Robinson* (Junior World Biographies series). Chelsea House, 1994. (For ages 9-12)

Crouchett, Lorraine J. *Delilah Leontium Beasley: Oakland's Crusading Journalist.* Downey Place, 1990. (Brief, adult level)

Ericsson, Mary K. *Morrie Turner, Creator of "Wee Pals".* Childrens Press, 1986. (For ages 9-12)

Ferris, Jeri Chase. *With Open Hands: A Story about Biddy Mason.* Carolrhoda Books, 1999. (For ages 8-12)

Gutman, Bill. *Tiger Woods: Golf's Shining Young Star.* Millbroo, 1998. (For ages 9-12)

Katz, William L. *Black Women of the Old West.* Atheneum, 1995. (For ages 10-14)

Koral, April. *Florence Griffith Joyner : Track and Field Star* (Full-Color First Books series). Watts, 1992. (For ages 9-12)

Schraff, Anne E. *Ralph Bunche : Winner of the Nobel Peace Prize* (African-American Biographies series). Enslow, 1999. (For ages 11-14)

Taylor, Quintard. *In Search of the Racial Frontier: African Americans in the American West, 1528-1990.* Norton, 1998. (Adult reading level)

Places to Visit

California African American Museum
> 600 State Dr., Exposition Park, Los Angeles 90037
> (213) 744-7432
> *www.caam.ca.gov*
> Web site has a biography section called Family Album, with photographs. There's a special Kids' Space with activities.

San Francisco African American Museum
> Fort Mason Center, Building C, San Francisco 94123
> (415) 441-0640
> *www.sfstation.com/museums/african.htm*

Center for African and African American Art and Culture
> 762 Fulton Street, San Francisco 94102
> (415) 928-8546
> *www.caaac.org*

National Civil Rights Museum in Memphis
> *www.civilrightsmuseum.org*
> Web site has an interactive tour highlighting individuals who played significant roles in the American civil rights movement.

The African American Mosaic : A Library of Congress
> Resource Guide for the Study of Black History and Culture.
> *lcweb.loc.gov/exhibits/african/afam001.html*